Dog Crafts

Written and Illustrated by
Linda Hendry

WITHDRAWN

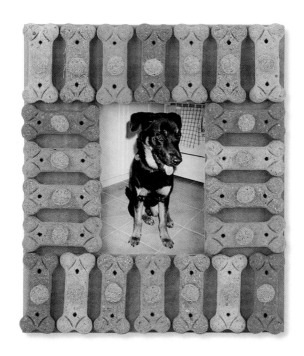

KIDS CAN PRESS

For Lady, Skipper and Duffy

Text and illustrations © 2002 Linda Hendry

KIDS CAN DO IT and the 🐾 logo are trademarks of Kids Can Press Ltd.

Kids Can Press acknowledges the support of the Government of Canada, through the BPIDP, for our publishing activity.

Published in Canada by
Kids Can Press Ltd.
29 Birch Avenue
Toronto, ON M4V 1E2

Published in the U.S. by
Kids Can Press Ltd.
2250 Military Road
Tonawanda, NY 14150

www.kidscanpress.com

Edited by Laurie Wark
Designed by Karen Powers
Photography by Frank Baldassarra
Printed in Hong Kong by Wing King Tong Company Limited

The hardcover edition of this book is smyth sewn casebound.
The paperback edition of this book is limp sewn with a drawn-on cover.

CM 02 0 9 8 7 6 5 4 3 2 1
CM PA 02 0 9 8 7 6 5 4 3 2 1

National Library of Canada Cataloguing in Publication Data

Hendry, Linda
Dog crafts

(Kids can do it)
Includes index.
ISBN 1-55074-960-9 (bound)   ISBN 1-55074-962-5 (pbk.)

1. Handicraft — Juvenile literature. 2. Dogs — Equipment and supplies — Juvenile literature. 3. Gifts — Juvenile literature. I. Title. II. Series.

SF427.15.H44 2002   j745.5   C2001-901700-6

Kids Can Press is a Nelvana company

Contents

Introduction

Knick, knack, paddy whack ...
give a dog (or a dog lover) a bone ...
or a dog biscuit frame, or a collar cover,
or a lampshade. Whether they are
four-legged and furry or your pals from
school, your friends will know how much
they mean to you when you make them
a special gift. This book will show you
how. While you are at it, why not
make a gift or two for yourself?

MATERIALS

These crafts are made from easy-to-fin
materials. Many supplies can be foun
around your home. A craft supply sto
should have the materials you need to
buy. Before you begin, cover your wo
surface with newspaper to protect it
from glue and paint.

Cardboard

Some projects require corrugated
cardboard or light cardboard.
Corrugated cardboard is used to mak
boxes for heavy things. Ask your groc
for a box. Crackers and dog biscuits
come in boxes made from light
cardboard.

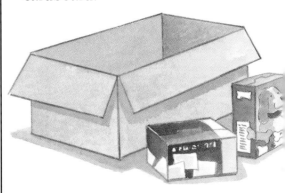

Glue

White, non-toxic glue is strong and
dries clear. Have a few clothespins or
hand when you are gluing. They can
often be used to hold pieces together
while they dry.

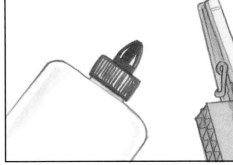

issors and utility knives

u can do most of the cutting in this ok with a pair of sharp scissors. If u are cutting cardboard or paper and uld like a straighter edge, use a ility knife and a metal-edged ruler. ways ask an adult to help you use a ility knife, and protect your working rface with a piece of corrugated rdboard.

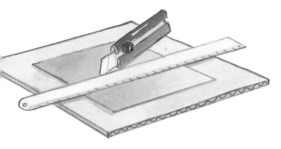

ints and paintbrushes

rylic craft paints come in lots of lors, and they give your project a ooth finish. They dry quickly, so place ly as much as you need onto a piece wax paper.

e a small pointed brush for painting tails. Flat straight-edged brushes can used for painting larger areas. Clean ur brushes with water before changing lor, and rinse them well when you are ished painting.

Sewing

To make the Puppy Pillow on page 16 and the Pooch Pencil Case on page 20, you must know how to do a blanket stitch. Follow the diagrams below.

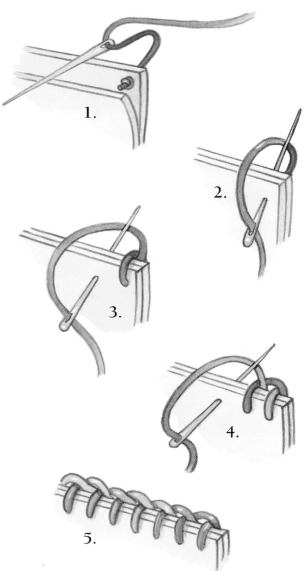

1.

2.

3.

4.

5.

Measuring

Measurements are given in both metric and imperial. Choose one measurement system and use it for the entire project.

My dog's photo album

If you have lots of photos to show off, make a few extra pages.

YOU WILL NEED

- bristol board, 6 black pieces each 14 cm x 20 cm (5½ in. x 8 in.), 2 green pieces each 18 cm x 22 cm (7 in. x 8½ in.)

- 2 pieces of yarn or string, each 30 cm (12 in.) long

- a pencil, scissors, masking tape, a ruler, a table knife, markers or crayons, a hole punch

- self-adhesive photo corners or tape

1 Place one piece of black bristol board on top of one piece of green, lining up the bottoms. Draw th dog shape on the green piece as show Set the black piece aside and cut out the shape.

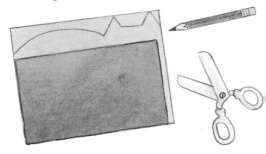

2 Trace the dog shape onto the second piece of green bristol board and cut it out. These are the covers.

3 On one piece of black bristol board, punch five evenly spaced holes along one short side. Using this as a pattern, trace the holes onto the remaining pieces of black bristol board and punch them out. These are the pages.

Place one page on a cover with the holes at the tail end of the dog ...ape as shown. Trace the holes and ...nch them out. Repeat this for the ...cond cover.

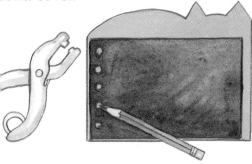

Wrap one end of each piece of yarn with a small piece of tape ...is will make it easier to sew with).

...ce the pages
...ween the
...vers and align
... holes.

...tch the
...um together
... shown.

... the ends of
... yarn with a
...uble knot.
...m.

6 Lay the ruler beside the holes on the front cover, and run the table knife along the ruler. Open the cover along the line.

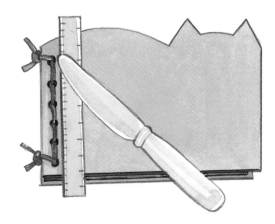

7 Color the front and back covers to look like a dog.

8 Use self-adhesive photo corners or tape to attach your photos to the pages.

Treat jars

Here are some fun ways to decorate a container for dog treats.

1 Arrange and trim the pictures to fit the jar and lid, then place the on newspaper and outline each pictu with the black marker.

Thin a spoonful of glue with
several drops of water. Brush it
to the back of the pictures, and
ach them to the jar and lid. Let the
ue dry, then seal with another coat of
e glue mixture.

THER IDEAS

e dimensional craft paint to outline
ch picture and draw designs onto the
at jar.

YOU WILL NEED

- a clean clear-plastic container
  with a lid
- 3 or 4 colors of dimensional
  craft paint

1 Draw designs on the jar and lid
with the dimensional paint. Do a
small section at a time, and let it dry
before continuing. (To avoid splatters,
occasionally tap the nozzle of the tube
on your work surface to remove air
bubbles.)

Handy hound hook

No more lost leashes! This helpful little hound will have them hooked.

YOU WILL NEED

- a piece of corrugated cardboard 13 cm x 15 cm (5 in. x 6 in.)
- an egg carton cup
- 2 sheets of paper towel
- a piece of coat-hanger wire 20 cm (8 in.) long
- small beads or buttons
- a piece of twine 13 cm (5 in.) long
- a pencil, scissors, masking tape, a spoon, white glue, a small bowl, paints, paintbrushes

1   Draw a pear shape on the corrugated cardboard and cut it out.

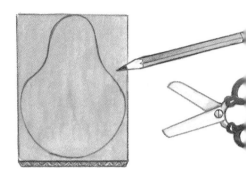

2   To make the nose, tape the egg carton cup near the center of the pear shape.

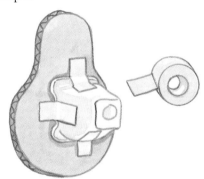

3   Tear off a strip of paper towel, roll it into a ball, and tape it to the egg carton as shown.

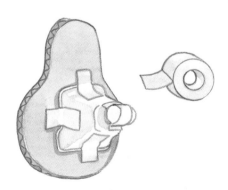

Bend the wire into a **U** shape, then bend up the lower part of ⎿e **U** to make a hook. Tape the hook ⎿ place.

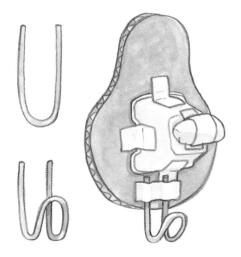

6 Paint the dog's face, then glue on two beads for eyes. Paint a collar, and glue on beads or buttons to decorate it.

Tear the rest of the paper towel into short strips. Mix two ⎿oonfuls of glue with one spoonful of ⎿ter, and brush the mixture onto a ⎿all section of the cardboard. Apply ⎿ paper towel strips to the glue and ⎿ush more glue on top. Cover the dog ⎿ several layers of glue mixture and ⎿per towel. Let it dry.

7 To hang the leash hook, make a loop with the twine and glue it to the back of the dog's head.

Dog biscuit frame

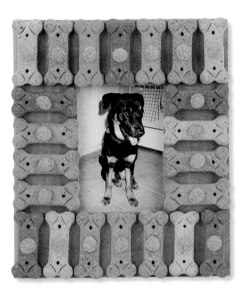

*This frame looks good enough to eat —
if you're a dog. Be sure to hang it
out of Fido's reach.*

YOU WILL NEED

- 2 pieces of corrugated cardboard, each about 25 cm x 30 cm (10 in. x 12 in.)
- 20 to 30 medium-sized dog biscuits
- 20 to 30 pieces of dog kibble
- a piece of light cardboard about 25 cm x 30 cm (10 in. x 12 in.)
- a piece of cord 13 cm (5 in.) long
- a pencil, a ruler, a utility knife or scissors, white glue
- paint and a paintbrush (optional)

1 On one piece of corrugated cardboard, lay out the dog biscui to form a frame. Draw a straight line around the frame, set the biscuits asid and cut out the frame.

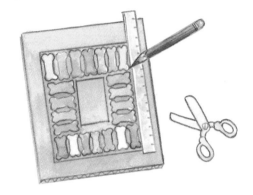

2 Paint the frame if you wish. Whe it is dry, glue the biscuits in plac Let the glue dry completely.

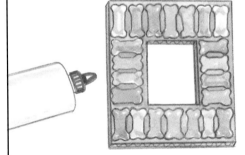

3 Glue a piece of kibble to the top of each biscuit. Let the glue dry completely.

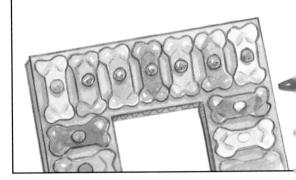

4 To make a backing for your frame, place it on the other piece corrugated cardboard and trace ound the outside. Cut out the shape.

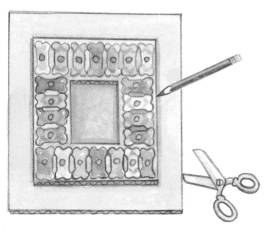

7 Run a line of glue along each cardboard strip, and glue the frame front to the backing.

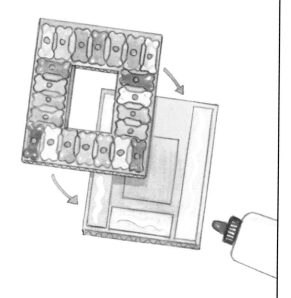

5 Trace the opening of e frame onto the cking piece, then move the front.

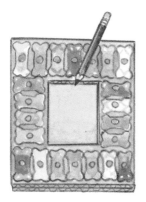

6 Cut three strips of light rdboard to fit the cking as shown. ue the strips in ce. These will act spacers and allow u to slide a photo o the frame.

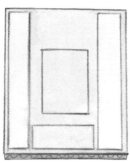

8 To hang your frame, make a loop with the cord and use plenty of glue to attach it securely to the back of the frame.

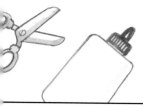

Key holder

Cup hooks, cardboard, glue and paint are all you need to make this great-looking key holder.

YOU WILL NEED

- corrugated cardboard,
  1 piece 5 cm x 13 cm (2 in. x 5 in.),
  2 pieces each 5 cm x 10 cm (2 in. x 4 in.),
  4 pieces each 5 cm x 23 cm (2 in. x 9 in.)
- 3 beads
- 3 4-cm (1 ½-in.) cup hooks
- a pencil, scissors, paints, paintbrushes, white glue, a hammer and 2 small nails

1 On the three smaller rectangles of cardboard, draw the dog shapes as shown.

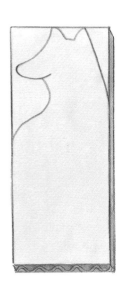
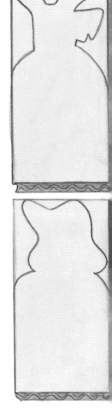

2 Cut out the dogs and paint them. Glue a bead onto each dog to create an eye.

To make the base, glue the four
strips of cardboard together.
hen the glue is dry, paint
base.

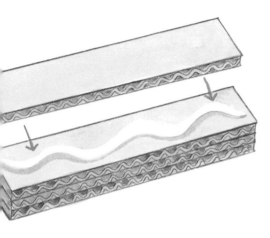

5 Screw a cup hook into each dog
to create a tail.

Glue the tallest dog to the center
of the base. Glue a shorter dog
cm (1 in.) from each end. Let the
e dry.

6 To hang your key holder, ask an
adult to hammer a nail through
each end of the base.

Puppy pillow

This furry fella is a doggone irresistible gift. Make one for your own bed, too!

YOU WILL NEED

- a piece of fuzzy felt or fleece 45 cm x 56 cm (18 in. x 22 in.)
- a piece of paper 45 cm x 28 cm (18 in. x 11 in.)
- embroidery floss or yarn and a darning needle
- fiberfill stuffing
- 2 black buttons
- a pencil, scissors, straight pins, a needle and thread

1 On the paper, draw the dog shap and ear pattern as shown and cut them out.

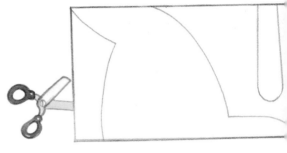

2 Fold the felt in half, right side out short sides together. Place the bottom of the pattern along the fold a pin it in place through both layers of felt. Pin the ear pattern and cut out th pieces. Do not cut along the fold. Remove the pins and patterns.

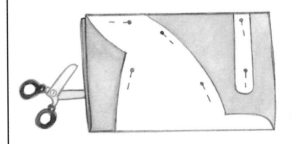

3 Place the ears, right sides together, on the body as shown. Fold up the body and pin all the layers to hold the ears in place.

Thread the darning needle with yarn. Starting at the tip of the tail, nket stitch (see page 5) along the tail d up the back of the dog to the ears. e a running stitch, as shown, to sew ross the ears, then continue to blanket tch until you have a 10 cm (4 in.) ening. Remove the pins.

Double knot the thread and push the needle through the eye area. Slide a button on, pass the needle back through the button and pull tight, creating an indent in the dog's face. Slide the other button onto the thread, and sew both buttons in place by passing the needle back and forth through them several times. Tie a double knot to finish. Trim.

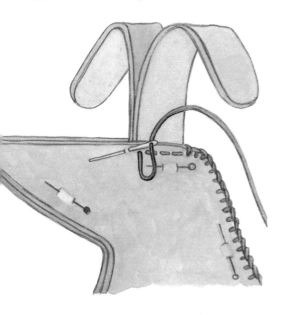

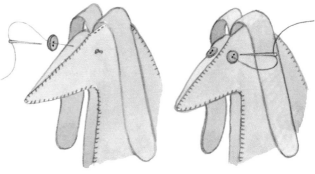

Use a pencil to push stuffing into the tail, then stuff the rest of the low until it is full. Sew up the ening using a blanket stitch.

Double knot a piece of yarn and push the needle through near the end of the nose. Wrap the yarn to the tip of the nose, passing under the blanket stitches to hold it in place. Tie a knot, then pull the needle back under the yarn to hide the knot. Trim.

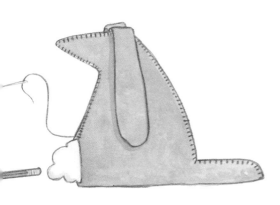

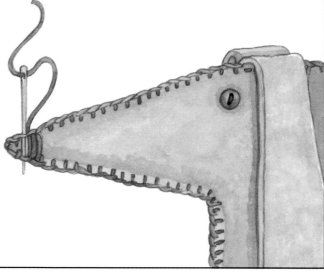

Switchplate cover

This is a fun way to jazz up a light switch!

YOU WILL NEED

- a switchplate cover and screws
- a piece of corrugated cardboard 12 cm x 16.5 cm (4½ in. x 6½ in.)
- scraps of colored paper
- pictures of dogs clipped from magazines
- a pencil, a ruler, a utility knife or scissors, a spoon, white glue, a small bowl, a paintbrush

1 If you are removing the switchplate cover from the wall, ask an adult to help. Do not lose the screws!

2 Place the switchplate in the center of the cardboard and draw around it. Remove the cover and draw a line 2 cm (¾ in.) inside each line you drew. Cut out the smaller rectangle and discard.

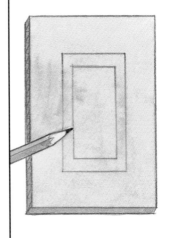

3 Draw a bone shape as shown and cut it out.

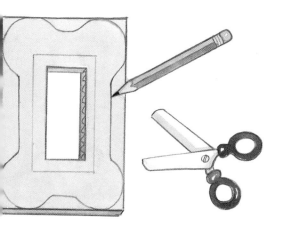

5 Glue the dog pictures onto the bone and seal with more glue mixture. Let the glue dry.

4 Mix five spoonfuls of glue with two spoonfuls of water, and brush some of the mixture onto a small section of the bone. Tear the scraps of paper into small strips, and apply them to the glue, wrapping them around the edges to the back of the cardboard. Brush more glue on top. Continue until the bone is covered. Let the glue dry.

6 Run a line of white glue near the edge of the switchplate cover, and attach the bone. When the glue is dry, ask an adult to screw the cover back in place.

Pooch pencil case

This pooch will keep your pencils in place.

YOU WILL NEED

• felt,
1 piece 14 cm x 20 cm (5½ in. x 8 in.),
1 piece 23 cm x 30 cm (9 in. x 12 in.),
1 small circle

• embroidery floss in 2 colors and
a darning needle

• 2 medium-sized buttons

• 1 small black craft pom-pom and
2 medium-sized pom-poms the same color

• 2 small beads

• straight pins, scissors, a needle and
thread, a pen, white glue

1 Make a fold 7.5 cm (3 in.) up from the bottom of the small piece of felt and pin it in place.

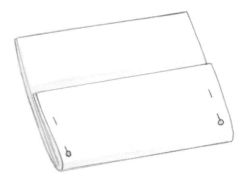

2 Using one color of embroidery floss and the darning needle, blanket stitch (see page 5) the sides together to create a pocket. Remove the pins.

3 To make the ears, trim the top of the felt pocket as shown. Turn the pocket over, fold the ears down and stitch them in place with thread.

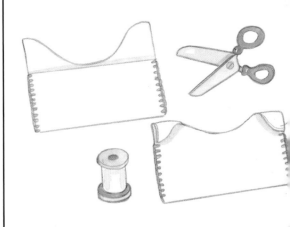

On the large
piece of felt,
ke a fold
cm (5 in.) up
m the bottom,
en turn the
ce over. Center
e pocket along
e folded edge
d pin it in
ce. Unfold the
ge piece and
ch the inside
the pocket to it
several places.
move the pins.

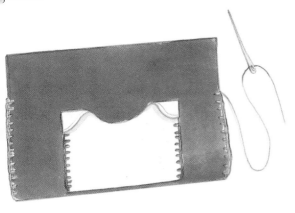

Refold the large piece of felt and
use the other color of embroidery
ss to blanket stitch the sides
ether.

6 On the flap, make two cuts that
are slightly shorter than the
buttons. Fold the flap down, and use a
pen to mark the center of each of these
button holes on the case.

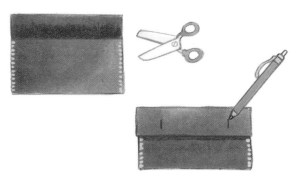

7 Open the flap and sew a button
securely to each spot you marked.

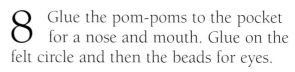

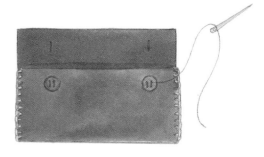

8 Glue the pom-poms to the pocket
for a nose and mouth. Glue on the
felt circle and then the beads for eyes.

Collar cover

Spiff up your dog's collar for special occasions or everyday wear.

1 Place the material wrong side down and fold under 1.5 cm (⅝ in.) at each end.

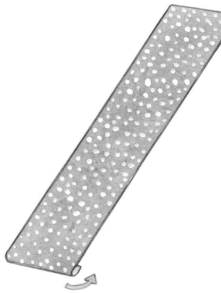

2 Fold the material in half, lining up the long edges. Pin it in place.

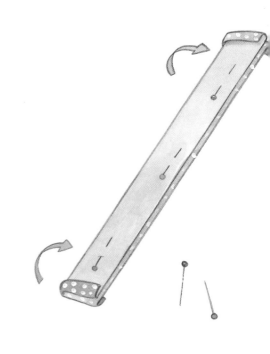

Leaving a 1 cm (½ in.) seam, sew along the edge with a running stitch as shown to make a tube.

Turn the tube right side out.

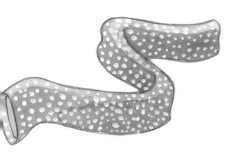

Sew the buttons to the top layer of fabric only. (To make this easier, first cut a strip of cardboard and slide it in the tube.)

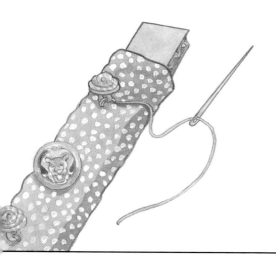

6 Holding the buckle, insert the collar into the tube and push the entire cover onto the collar.

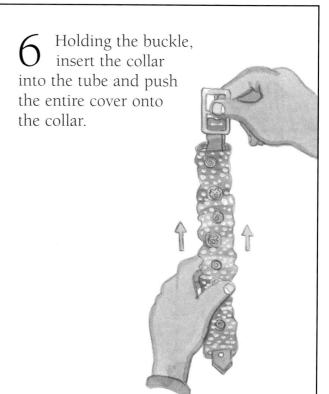

7 Fasten the collar on your dog and even out the cover.

Safety tip
Remember to check regularly for loose buttons, and fix them right away.

Puppy-dog placemat

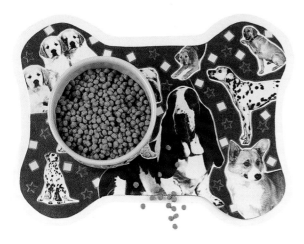

*Give a dog a bone-shaped placemat,
and make cleaning up after a
messy eater a breeze!*

YOU WILL NEED

- a piece of newsprint
30 cm x 40 cm (12 in. x 16 in.)
- a piece of bristol board
30 cm x 40 cm (12 in. x 16 in.)
- pictures of dogs, photocopied or
clipped from magazines
- colorful stickers or
shapes cut from paper (optional)
- 2 sheets of clear, self-adhesive vinyl,
each 35 cm x 45 cm (14 in. x 18 in.)
- a pencil, scissors, a glue stick

1 To make the pattern, fold the
newsprint in half, long sides
together, and draw half of a bone shape
as shown. Cut out the pattern.

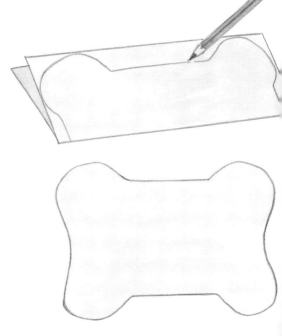

2 Unfold the pattern and trace it
onto the bristol board. Cut out
the placemat.

3 Put the dog pictures and stickers on the placemat. When you like the design, glue the pictures in place. Trim any that stick over the edge.

5 Peel back one long edge of the other sheet of vinyl and carefully line it up with one long edge of the first piece. Smooth out the vinyl and peel away a bit more of the backing. Continue to smooth the vinyl and remove the backing until the entire sheet is in place.

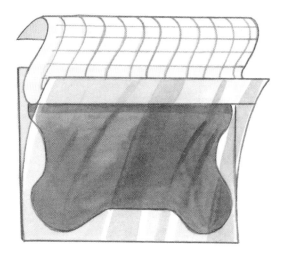

4 Peel the backing paper off one sheet of vinyl. With the picture side down, center the placemat on the vinyl. Press firmly and smooth out the placemat.

6 Turn the placemat over. Smooth out any wrinkles or bubbles, then trim the placemat, leaving a small margin of vinyl around the edges.

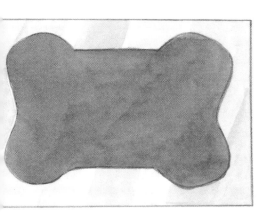

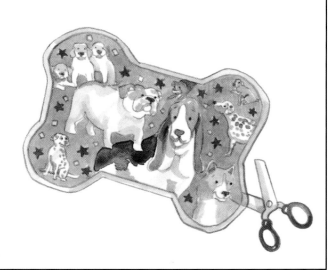

Doggy desktop organizer

Here's a pack of pooches to guard your pencils and keep your desktop tidy.

YOU WILL NEED

- about 6 light cardboard boxes of various shapes and sizes
- pictures of dogs, photocopied or clipped from magazines
- several pieces of light cardboard
- scissors, white glue, several clothespins, paints, paintbrushes

1 Trim the boxes if necessary, and arrange them into a design you like. When you are happy with your arrangement, glue the boxes together. Hold them in place with the clothespins until they are dry.

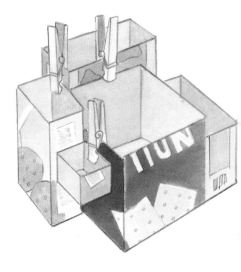

2 To create compartments, glue one or two smaller boxes inside a larger box.

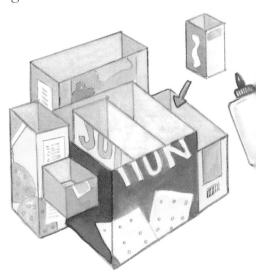

3 Paint the boxes and let them dry.

5 Glue the dogs to the boxes, holding them in place with the clothespins until they are dry.

4 Glue each dog picture onto the printed side of a piece of light rdboard. Trim around the image, int the back of the cardboard, and it dry.

6 Paint a pattern on the parts of the boxes not covered by the dogs.

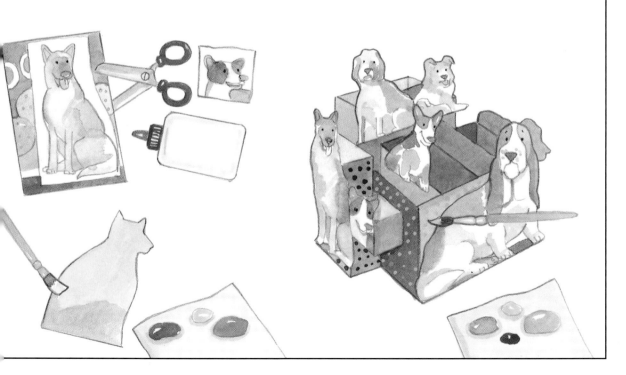

Grooming caddy

Transform a shoe box into a storage caddy with four handy compartments.

YOU WILL NEED

- a shoe box
- a corrugated cardboard box larger than the shoe box
- a piece of cord 1½ times the length of the shoe box
- a ruler, a utility knife or scissors, a pencil, white glue, masking tape, paints, paintbrushes, a hole punch

1 From the corrugated cardboard, cut two pieces the same length as the long side of the shoe box and 4 cm (1½ in.) taller.

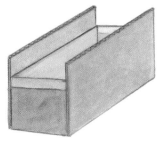

2 Cut two pieces of cardboard the same length as the short side of the shoe box and 9 cm (3½ in.) taller.

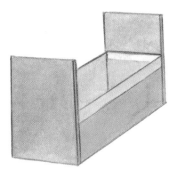

3 Mark the center point on each piece from step 2 as shown, then make a mark 5 cm (2 in.) down on each side. Draw a line from the center point to each mark, and cut along the lines.

4 Glue the cardboard pieces to the sides of the shoe box, and cover each corner with tape.

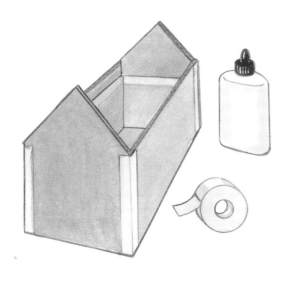

5 To make the compartments, cut two strips of cardboard to fit inside the shoe box from corner to corner.

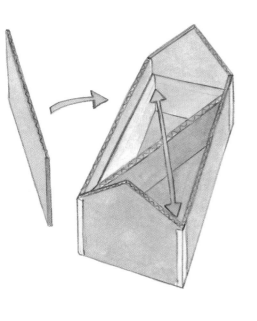

6 At the center of each strip, make a cut halfway through. Slide the strips together to form an **X**. Set the strips inside the box to make four compartments.

7 Paint the shoe box, and let it dry. Punch a hole in each end, thread the cord through, and tie a knot in each end to form a handle.

Canine clipboard

This pooch will keep an eye on your papers!

- corrugated cardboard,
1 piece 10 cm x 45 cm (4 in. x 18 in.),
4 pieces each 4 cm x 8 cm (1½ in. x 3 in.),
1 piece 13 cm x 13 cm (5 in. x 5 in.)

- 2 pieces of light cardboard,
each 4 cm x 8 cm (1½ in. x 3 in.)

- 4 wooden clothespins, painted

- paints, paintbrushes, a pencil, scissors,
white glue, a hammer and 2 small nails

1 Paint a checkered pattern on the long strip of cardboard. Set it aside to dry.

2 Following the steps below, draw dog shape on the 13 cm x 13 cm (5 in. x 5 in.) piece of cardboard. Cut out the dog shape and paint it. Set it aside to dry.

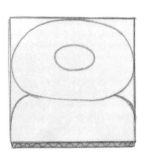

3 To make the ears, fold each piece of light cardboard as shown, and ut off the corners. Paint the ears and t them dry. Glue the ears to the dog.

4 Draw a sausage shape on each of the four small pieces of rdboard. Cut them out, paint them, d set them aside to dry.

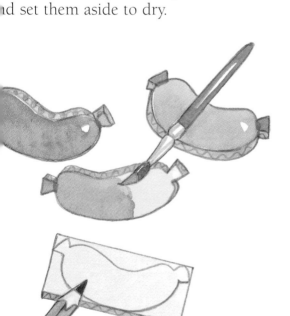

5 Glue the dog to the center of the checkered strip. Glue two clothespins on either side of the dog as shown. Let the glue dry.

6 Glue a sausage near the top of each clothespin.

7 To hang your clipboard, ask an adult to hammer a nail through each end of the checkered strip.

Dangly dog jewelry

Once you've made these earrings, make a matching necklace and thread a cord through the loop. Or omit the loop and create a brooch by attaching a pin back.

YOU WILL NEED

- Fimo or other polymer clay in white, black and brown
- 4 7-mm (5/16-in.) jump rings
- 2 shepherd hooks (ear wires)
- a table knife, a needle, a baking sheet, tin foil, needlenose pliers

1 Use your finger to flatten two marble-sized pieces of brown clay into circles about 0.25 cm (1/8 in.) thick.

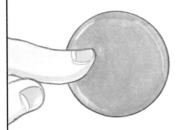

2 Roll a pea-sized ball of brown clay into a log about 8 cm (3 in.) long. Cut the log in half and form each piece into a loop. Attach a loop to the back each earring, at the top of each circle.

3 Flatten two pea-sized balls of brown clay, and press one onto each circle.

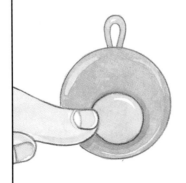

4 Roll two small balls of black clay into cylinders, and press one onto each small brown circle to make a nose.

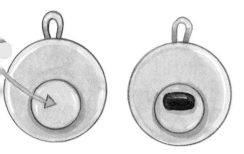

5 Use the knife to make a small cut under each nose, then poke three holes on either side of the cut with the needle.

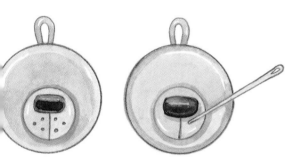

6 Press four pea-sized balls of black into teardrop shapes, then press two teardrops onto each circle to make ears. Fold down the top of each teardrop shape.

7 To make the eyes, press a tiny ball of white onto each teardrop shape and poke a hole in the center of each with the needle.

8 With an adult's help, bake the earrings on a foil-lined baking sheet according to the directions on the packages of clay. When the earrings are cool, use the pliers to carefully attach two jump rings and a shepherd hook to each loop.

Accessory organizer

Get along, little doggie, and organize your jewelry and hair accessories.

1 Glue three small strips of cardboard together. Repeat to ma another three-layer strip. Set the piece aside to dry. These are spacers.

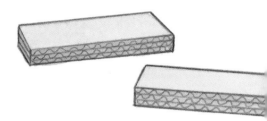

2 On the large piece of cardboard, draw the dog's body and cut it o

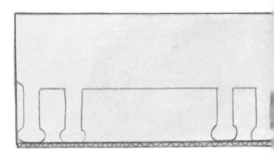

3 Draw the head on the medium-sized cardboard and cut it out.

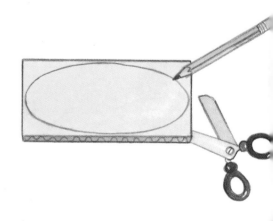

4 On the remaining strip of cardboard, draw a tail and cut it out.

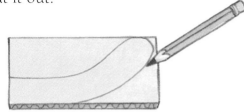

5 Glue the head to the front of the body and the tail to the back. Let them dry, then paint the dog.

6 To make pockets, cut two large felt spot shapes and run a line of glue around the sides and bottom of each. Attach them to the dog.

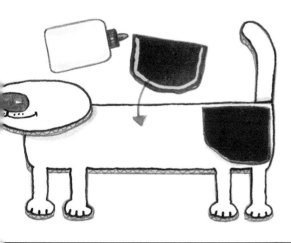

7 Cut two small felt spots and glue them to the dog's head. Glue a bead on each spot to make eyes. Cut long, thin felt ear shapes. Glue one to the front of the head and one to the back.

8 Glue the spacers to the back. They will hold your organizer away from the wall so you can attach clips and slide accessories onto the legs.

9 To attach your organizer to the wall, ask an adult to hammer a nail through each spacer.

Doghouse bookend

To make a set of bookends, double the amount of materials you will need.

YOU WILL NEED

- a clean, large milk or juice container
- light cardboard
  (such as a cereal box)
- sandpaper
- a piece of corrugated cardboard about 15 cm x 20 cm (6 in. x 8 in.)
- 375 mL (1½ c.) sand or small pebbles
- a small plastic bag
- an empty toilet paper tube
- a scrap of black paper
- scissors, a pencil, white glue, masking tape, clothespins, paints, paintbrushes

1 Cut the milk container in half. A[t] each corner of the bottom half, make two cuts as shown. Remove the cut sections and set the bottom aside.

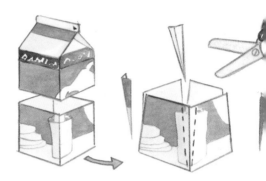

2 Trace each side of the top half of the container onto a piece of lig[ht] cardboard. Cut out the shapes.

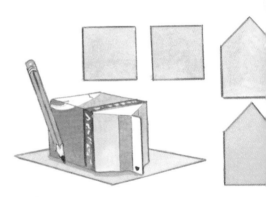

3 Sand the sides and top of the container with the sandpaper. Glue the cardboard shapes to the side[s] and cover the edges with tape.

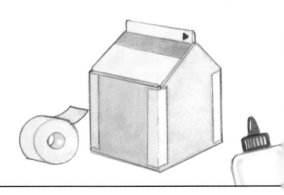

4 To make a roof, cut and fold a piece of light cardboard to fit over the top of the container and overlap the sides. Apply glue and hold the roof in place with clothespins until it is dry.

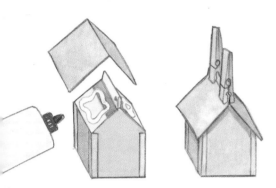

5 Paint the container to look like a doghouse.

6 Paint the corrugated cardboard green. When the paint is dry, sand the bottom half of the container and glue it to the cardboard as shown.

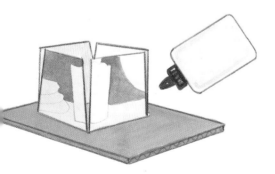

7 Pour the sand into the plastic bag and tie a knot. Set the bag inside the bottom half of the container. Slide the top half over the bottom.

8 To make the dog, cut the tube in half, then cut the head and legs as shown.

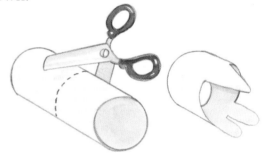

9 Tape over the tube opening and paint the dog. Cut two ears from the black paper, and glue them on. Glue the dog in front of the doghouse.

Decorated lampshade

If your lampshade is smaller or larger, adjust the number and position of the dogs to fit, or try making your own designs!

YOU WILL NEED

- a white, cloth-covered hardback lampshade, about 30 cm (12 in.) across the bottom and 20 cm (8 in.) high
- black dimensional fabric paint
- a black marker and tracing paper, scissors, masking tape, a pencil, paints, paintbrushes

1   Photocopy — or use the marker and tracing paper to trace — three copies of each pattern on page 40. Cut out the patterns.

2   Tape one pattern (drawing side face down) to the inside of the lampshade, close to the side seam and along the bottom edge.

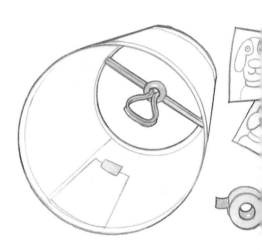

3   Tape the second pattern about 8 cm (3 in.) from the first. Continue taping the patterns to the inside of the lampshade, alternating the patterns and spacing them evenly.

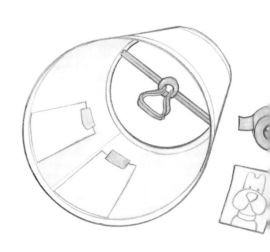

4 Check your design. If you can't see the patterns clearly, hold the shade up to a light. When you are happy with the design, trace the patterns onto the lampshade with the pencil. Remove the patterns.

5 Carefully paint the dogs and let them dry.

6 Outline the dogs with the dimensional fabric paint. (To avoid splatters, occasionally tap the nozzle of the tube on your work surface to remove air bubbles.) Do only one or two dogs at a time and let them dry so you don't smudge them.

7 Carefully draw a line of fabric paint along the top and bottom edges of the lampshade. Let the paint dry.

OTHER IDEAS

Make holes along the bottom edge of the shade with a hole punch. Make dog bones from polymer clay, and tie a bone to each hole.

Lampshade patterns (for page 38)

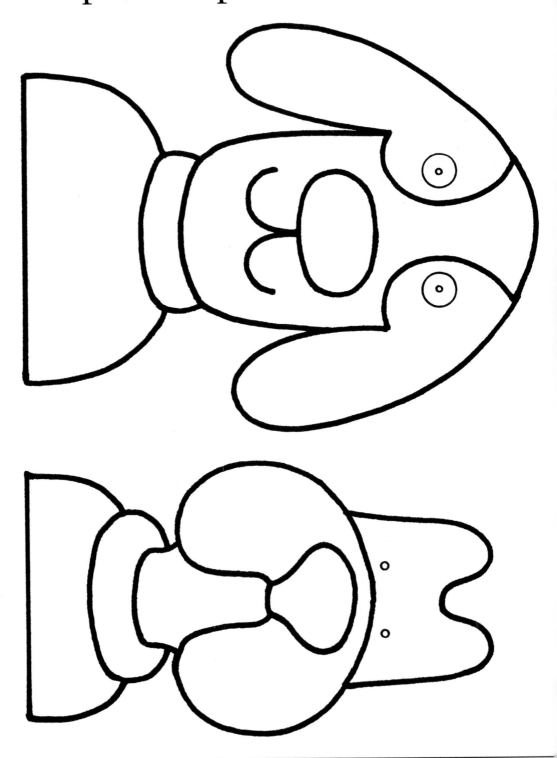